sk

sh

d

lip

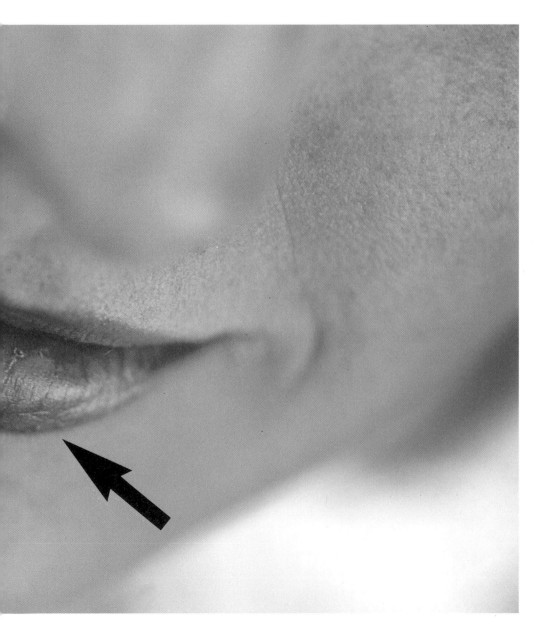

zip

Here are some activities you can do with your young reader.

1. Have your child look through the book to find the picture of the girl skipping. Brainstorm with your child, words that end with **-ip**, such as **hip** and **chip**. Write each word on a separate sheet of paper. Then tape the sheets of paper to the floor, placing them several feet apart. As you say each word aloud, have your child **skip** to the appropriate word.

2. Explain to your child that the word **rip** ends with the **-ip** sound. Then gather a variety of papers, including paper towels, construction paper, and newspaper. Together, rip each paper item in half and then tear off tiny pieces. On a sheet of construction paper, glue the paper pieces in the shape of an **-ip** word, such as **zip**.

3. Reread the rhyme, inviting your child to touch the **tip** of his or her nose each time he or she hears a word ending with **-ip**. Then discuss the different kinds of acts that are performed in a circus. Invite your child to illustrate one of the circus acts.

Steck-Vaughn
Phonics
Build-A-Word ™
Books

Zip, Flip, and Dip!

Watch how the acrobats
Zip through the air!
They turn and they flip.
They twist and they dip.
They grip the bar tightly.
They don't want to slip!
The excited crowd watches.
Their hearts skip a beat.
"Hip, hip, hooray!" they yell
From their seats.

STECK-VAUGHN
A Harcourt Company

ISBN 0-7398-4597-7

9 780739 845974
90000